REGINALD BEAN

UNFINISHED

40 LESSONS
ON PURPOSE, SELF,
AND BECOMING A MAN

Published by Reginald Bean

Design and production by SPARK Publications
www.SPARKpublications.com

Printing History
Edition One, June 2013

ISBN: 978-0-615-78185-3

Unfinished: 40 Lessons on Purpose, Self, and Becoming a Man

DEDICATION

The book is dedicated to young men with the desire to be productive and responsible in leading their families and impacting their communities.

This book is also dedicated to the two women who helped shape me into the man I am today. My Grandmother, Anne Margaret Brooks, and my Mother, Angela Brooks. Both women taught me the value of hard work and perseverance, and the benefits of continuous learning.

TABLE OF CONTENTS

THE MOTIVATION

In traveling across this country and around the world I have had the pleasure of meeting a wide range of young men. I've witnessed young men celebrate in Seoul, South Korea and struggle in Oakland, California. My journey put me up close and personal with some of the brightest young men whose full potential was simply never reached. My conclusion: men, young and old, lack basic awareness and understanding of their impact on their environment.

Simply put many of us men don't understand that we are the cause and cure! Absence in our kids' lives causes in them low self-esteem, little or no discipline and difficulty listening to and obeying authority figures. On the other hand, our presence is the cure! The cure is instilling confidence and setting expectations for structure and discipline in addition to teaching our children what it feels like to be loved unconditionally.

Men play a vital role in the success and failure of our children, wives, and communities. The reality is we never set a goal to fail our families and communities. That's never the goal to start with, but it happens. It happens with our lack of presence. It happens with our lack of preparation with our children, by failing to arm them with basic character skills and an environment of structure, stability and love.

Many of us enter into adulthood with more training on iPads, smartphones, and operating cars compared to the basic skills and understanding of our roles and responsibilities as men.

In the environment in which I grew up, the concept of preparing a boy for manhood was taboo and didn't exist. This lack of preparation led to an atmosphere full of young men who did not understand the idea of accountability or that there were expectations for raising boys to become productive men. I look back over the early years of my life and I wish I'd had someone to advise me on the road ahead. I honestly think I would have listened.

I hope my stories of happiness, poor judgment, mistakes, and mishaps will help you avoid similar pitfalls. Most importantly, my goal is to help you understand in great detail that your role as a productive and responsible man is essential to your family and community.

This book is not simply to be read. It is to be experienced by comparing and contrasting my stories and journey with yours. The goal is not to remind you how bad your life is or how much you have messed up. We've all messed up from time to time. I simply want to motivate you to discover your purpose and reach your full potential as a man, allowing you to strengthen your family and community. I encourage you to be honest while participating in the exercises; expressing your thoughts and feeling with each topic. Our journeys may not be exactly the same, but the necessity to provide structure, stability, and love for our families and communities is the same. ▪

What people are saying about
UNFINISHED

"By sharing his own personal experiences, Reginald has provided an authentic and applicable view into how we can all live rewarding and purposeful lives. His transparency and commitment to serving others is inspiring."
  — **Kevin Alan Henry,** SVP and Chief Human Resource Officer,
Snyder's-Lance,
Philanthropist and Community Leader

"Inspiring, uplifting, and the playbook for a young man trying to overcome life's challenges. **Unfinished** serves its purpose as the blueprint for me as I transition into adulthood."
  — **William Kannady**, Student, UNC Charlotte

"I have worked with male felons for over twenty-five years and one widely held perspective that many of them share is a sense of feeling 'alienated' from the 'mainstream society.' Over the years, several of them spoke about how feeling 'disconnected' impeded their ability to achieve their full potential; mainly because of a lack of knowledge about how to 'connect the dots' and work toward self-realization. **Unfinished** will serve as a guide for young men as they are reintroduced into society."
  — **Angela Brooks**, Probation Officer,
Michigan Department of Corrections

1

UNFINISHED
THE POTENTIAL TO BE GREAT

I grew up in Detroit in the '80s and '90s. Detroit is a city known for its blue-collar work force, no nonsense mentality and years of producing America's best automobiles. Detroit is also known for producing some of the most memorable musical talent for decades with the Motown sound. With its economic success, Detroit was also known for its violent and criminally infested streets, ranking among the top 1 or 2 cities in America for number of homicides for many years. These characteristics made it a breeding ground for physically aggressive and irresponsible behavior for young African American men. I was influenced by this exciting and often dangerous environment.

I, like many young men in Detroit, lacked the positive influence of my father, who decided that raising his son wasn't important. This often left me feeling unloved, unwanted, and angry.

Having my influences come from the streets opened the door for me to participate in unproductive behavior such as stealing, hanging with neighborhood drug dealers, underage drinking, and drug usage. Even though this type of behavior was and continues to be normal for the environment in Detroit, I always knew there was more I could have been pursuing with my life. Said differently, I knew I wasn't being who I was at my core. Fortunately, there were responsible men in my sights, like Mr. Orlowski (10th grade Civics Teacher), Mr. Johnson (11th grade English teacher), and Daryl 'Sir Nose' Ounanian (Youth Pastor), who reminded me that there were other options in life.

The inspiration for this book was the realization and understanding that life is a journey that never ends. I am continuously evolving as a man and will never truly "cross a finish line." I am like an unfinished portrait whose potential and greatness is continuously revealing itself. My inspirations have come from moments of celebration and defeat, but the portrait is continuously evolving.

You may have experiences similar to mine. You may be from New York, California, or North Carolina and face the same challenges. Whether we're rich, poor, black, or white none of us have it completely together. So don't be so anxious; take a little time to appreciate the scenery along the journey. Appreciate every chapter of life. As you grow up, don't be in such a rush that you neglect the details. Real joy is in the details of life.

If you accomplish something today, celebrate yourself. If you've lost a loved one, mourn your loss and then move forward after having taken some time to regroup. But remember you are evolving everyday on a journey that never ends. ■

CHALLENGE

We are all works in progress. Enjoy it. Embrace it. Don't feel forced to finish anything that you still need time to process. When you graduate, go on a small vacation or treat your self to some ice cream. There is nothing wrong with celebrating the milestones of your life. The more we celebrate, the more we are better able to balance life and balance our time.

EXERCISE

_____reminds me that I am a work in progress.

I struggle with _____
_____most times no matter how hard I work at it.

I can see myself being _____
_____once the artwork is complete.

"Be more concerned with your

character than your reputation,

because your character is what

you really are, while your

reputation is merely what

others think you are."

John Wooden

2

GROW BEYOND COMFORT
STEP OUTSIDE YOUR COMFORT ZONE

When I served in the Army, some of my friends were nothing like me. They were from different parts of the country with totally different backgrounds. They looked different, they acted differently and they thought differently from the way I'd always thought.

I remember one guy from Oklahoma City, he was a great guy, but he looked nothing like me! I was a laid-back kid from Detroit. He, on the other hand, looked like he had just finished filming a western movie. He wore tight jeans and cowboy boots while I sported the latest urban gear. He couldn't care less what name brand he wore. His club of choice was different than the club where my friends and I would hang out.

So, most times when he would invite me to hang out, I would look at his outfit and turn him down. "Sorry, man, I have plans tonight." I didn't give him a chance. Why? I was uncomfortable stepping outside of what I considered normal.

It took me a while to really "get" him, but once I did, we became great friends. Our journeys were different, but once I opened myself up to him, I was shocked to realize how much we actually had in common!

If I had allowed myself to remain uncomfortable with the unknown I would have missed out on a life-long friend. His friendship taught me a valuable lesson: never judge a book by its cover.

Many times we tend to hold on to what is familiar to us and we expect others to conform to us rather than understanding others for who they are. If we live life with a closed mind, we will never grow beyond what is comfortable and familiar to us.

Here's how I've learned to live my life: I don't let my comfort with what is normal to me stop me from experiencing what is abnormal to me. Try it yourself. Don't let your comfortable boundaries keep you from traveling into another neighborhood, exploring another city, or experiencing food from another country. Be open to growth! Most times, the things we fear most are the things we don't know. Don't let fear of the unknown keep you from living a life full of new experiences. ▪

CHALLENGE

Drop your invisible barriers. Step outside of your comfort zone.

EXERCISE

The Challenge Checklist:

☐ Try golf

☐ Try tennis

☐ Eat sushi

☐ Watch a foreign movie

(Add your own "something different.")

_____

_____

_____

_____

_____

_____

" We are not the same and we shouldn't expect others to behave and think like we do. Accepting others for who they are and what they bring to our lives ensures us that the true friend shows up. "

3

ONE OF US IS NOT LIKE THE OTHER
EXPECTATIONS OF OTHERS

Many people say I have a Type A personality. They describe me as super organized, brutally honest, sometimes impatient; I can become obsessed with time management and most importantly, I like to get to the point.

I don't know if I'm Type A or not, but a lot of these characteristics define the way I behave. I am very competitive. I want things to be in order. I want people to do what they say, and I need people to do things efficiently. If I'm at the park playing ball or if I'm in the library studying for a test, I want to be the best. I expect nothing less than the best for myself, and by default, I expect nothing but the best from everyone around me.

Well that's where it got a little muddy in my life.

It wasn't bad to have expectations for myself—I would think everyone should have personal goals and ambitions—but when I started to treat others with the same expectations, it really messed up my friendships. It got to the point where I stopped listening to anyone who didn't live up to my expectations.

My personality and unspoken expectations made other people around me feel uncomfortable. They felt rushed. They felt "weird." And it took me a long time to realize that they weren't me! They had their own strengths, habits, and styles. God made them differently...and that was O.K.

Eventually, people stopped feeling comfortable just being themselves around me. They stopped opening up about how they really felt, and, while they never said it, I could tell that they didn't want to be around me.

For somebody who wanted to think he had it together, that was hard to admit! I had hardly anything together. I had to learn that we are all different. Just because something works for me, doesn't mean you should try it too. I learned that each of us has things that we are good at and some things that we aren't so good at. Here's the reality: We are not the same and we shouldn't expect others to behave and think like we do. Accepting others for who they are and what they bring to our lives ensures us that the true friend shows up. ∎

CHALLENGE

Be cool with people who don't have the same personality as you. Don't expect them to be just like you. If you invite people into your circle, don't resist their differences. Allow others to be themselves. The bonus is that then you get to be yourself.

EXERCISE

Name some friends who have felt weird around you.

_____

_____

_____

_____

_____

_____

What expectations did you have that made them feel that way?

_____

_____

_____

_____

_____

_____

> **"**Nobody starts out running their fastest time or lifting their max weight. Nobody starts out stronger than they will ever become. It's preparation and hard work that separate us from everyone else.**"**

4

PREPARE FOR YOUR MOMENT
PREPARATION IS KEY

Imagine being a football player on the night of the NFL draft. You're sitting there with friends and family. Everyone is waiting for your name to be called. You would love to be selected by your favorite team but at this point you're thinking, "just give me any team." You have waited for this moment since you first stepped onto a football field at the age of 10.

Your mind flashes back to every practice, every win, and every loss. You've poured everything you've got into countless hours of practice. You've listened to coach after coach telling you what to do and how to do it. They forced you to do drill after drill, over and over until they were perfected. You've studied the playbook. You've turned down hanging with friends just to prepare yourself, and you've improved year by year. You worked hard and, yeah, you made sacrifices!

One day in college, the coach gave you great news…you were starting the game! From that moment, you never looked back. You took advantage of every moment and worked hard to improve your skills.

That announcement finally comes: You have been selected to the NFL! You have practiced continuously, studied the playbook front to back and dreamt about this moment and how you would respond. You prepared for your moment of opportunity.

Listen: Nobody starts out running their fastest time or lifting their max weight. Nobody starts out stronger than they will ever become. It's preparation and hard work that separate us from everyone else.

Throughout our lives we will be presented with opportunities, some at the most unexpected times and places. It may be the football field or the classroom. Once you have discovered your passion, you must put in countless hours to prepare for your moment. ▪

CHALLENGE

Opportunities don't present themselves and allow you to prepare; you have to prepare before the opportunities show up. If you're serious about your passion, make good use of every moment off the field or behind the stage, when no one can see you, and when you find yourself alone. In preparation, every moment counts.

EXERCISE

Actions you can take:
Write down your dreams for the future.

_____

_____

_____

_____

_____

_____

Now write down the things you're going to do to prepare for the day when opportunity shows up.

_____

_____

_____

_____

_____

" Everyone will not make the journey with you. It will take courage for you to live out your true purpose in the face of what others have to say about your decision. "

5

HAVE THE COURAGE TO BECOME YOURSELF
ACCEPTING WHO YOU ARE

When I was 14, my first summer job was working at a carwash. About a week into the job, I realized that we took a long time to wash each car. I wanted to reorganize the car washing process to save time. Instead of randomly washing cars, I wanted everyone to start at the top of the car, taking advantage of the suds running down the sides and saving water and time in the process. Then I wanted us to go down the chain with each person focusing on one particular part of the car. They listened! This new process allowed us to wash more cars throughout the day.

A similar thing happened when I was 16 and working at a famous fried chicken restaurant. I started as a regular employee, but soon enough, I found myself trying to improve processes in the kitchen just like I did at the car wash. I suggested to the manager that everyone learn multiple jobs so that no one became dependent on the cook. Besides, he would often show up late during rush hour, and our customers would get upset. I like improving things. Always have.

Imagine knowing that you have talents and dreams but are too ashamed to reveal them. Ashamed that your friends and family will look at you as the different one. This was my story. I was gifted but not courageous enough to be myself. I knew I had different talents than my friends and cousins, and I never felt like I fit in. My interest in reading didn't allow me to fit in. I dressed differently and I didn't fit in. I wanted to learn continuously and I didn't fit in.

Eventually, I began to let everyone in on who I was and my worst fears came true: teasing from my friends. They would tease me for wanting to do something different. I didn't realize it then, but each day would require courage on the journey of becoming everything I was created to be.

We can all be bold and courageous in who we are! Beginning a new journey oftentimes forces us to leave our pack of friends and invest in ourselves. But that's O.K. Everyone will not make the journey with you. It will take courage for you to live out your true purpose in the face of what others have to say about your decision. Whatever you do, don't deny or suppress your dreams or your talents just to stay with the crew. Be you! Be courageous! Don't waver! ■

CHALLENGE

Take the time to discover what's different about you. That's the first part of the process. Use your differences to set you apart. Be courageous and triumph over the ridicule.

EXERCISE

I'm afraid that if my friends found out_____

_____they would tease me.

I try to hide_____

_____talent because I think my friends will laugh.

_____

_____

was a time that I showed enough courage to be me.

" People don't always listen to

what you say; they watch what you do.

Your actions define your name. "

6

YOUR ACTIONS DEFINE YOUR NAME
THINK BEFORE YOU ACT

Many of us have that teenage story about doing something ridiculous to fit it with the guys. Mine happened when I was 15 years old.

My mother sent my brother and me to the mall to pick up some hair care products. We picked up a neighborhood friend along the way. When we got to the mall, my buddy dared me to steal something from the store.

Keep in mind, my mom was a mother of three boys and worked extremely hard to provide for us. We didn't have a lot, but she did a great job of providing the basics. But was I thinking about my mom's hard work at that moment and the potential outcome if I was caught? No.

I accepted the challenge, walked into the department store, took off a pair of my shoes and replaced them with a pair from the store. Fool that I was, I thought, "This is going to be an easy dare." I proceeded to walk out of the store.

Unbeknownst to me, an undercover security guard was following me a few steps behind. As I crossed the threshold of the store, he grabbed one arm and slapped handcuffs on the other. You can't imagine the disappointment from my family when they found out about my arrest.

That day taught me something crucial: People don't always listen to what you say; they watch what you do. Your actions define your name.

Stealing wasn't who I was. But for the next 24 months, I had to work to rebuild my name. Whenever I left the house, I had to understand that my mom would second-guess the details of my whereabouts. If I came home with new clothes, I had to explain two or three times to my mom where the items came from.

The credibility I had built with my family until that point was washed away. I had to allow my actions and locations to be questioned until the trust was rebuilt with my mom. I had to prove over and over again through consistent and trusting behavior that I was trustworthy and not a thief. Your actions truly define your name. ▪

CHALLENGE

When making hasty decisions, make sure you think about the potential outcome. What impression will you leave on your family? How will people think of you after you graduate? Don't just think for the now; think about the future.

EXERCISE

What is your ridiculous teenage story?

_____

_____

_____

_____

_____

_____

When was a time that you had to rebuild the trust of friends or family members?

_____

_____

_____

_____

_____

_____

" Whatever you do, don't allow

your thoughts to become bland.

Diversify yourself. Add spice

to your life. It doesn't matter where

you come from, the right recipe can

change your life forever. "

7

DIVERSIFY YOUR THOUGHTS
ADD NEW FLAVORS

I love to cook. I tend to think that I can throw down in the kitchen! When I served in the Army, my job for many years was as a Food Service specialist. I was taught to cook using basic seasonings for consistency with dishes. Eventually I began trying different seasoning and variations from the recipe. Experimenting with different recipes showed me how something that tasted so regular could be transformed into an amazing dish by simply adding a few new ingredients. These experiments in cooking taught me several lessons in preparation for life.

Imagine cooking and only having salt and pepper at your disposal. The menu would be pretty bland, don't you think? I mean, some people love salt and pepper, but those aren't the only seasoning options.

These lessons taught me not to be afraid of variety. Many of us live our lives the way our parents or relatives lived their lives: one way, with one pattern and one mindset. We drive down the same roads, we visit the same places, and we eat the same foods. But what new things could life have in store if we just added a little flavor to them?

Life gets exciting when we try new things, have new thoughts and visit new places. It is then, when we have added variety to something, that we see life in a different way.

If your life is bland, spice it up in a productive way. If it's too spicy, dilute some of the spice and tone it down a little. Trying one new book, one unique experience, or one new conversation could be the ingredient you need to change things! That's what adding diversity to your life and your thoughts is all about. Anyone who wants to be impactful in life has to understand that he will need to change things up and add new ingredients from time to time. Wear a different outfit. See a different kind of movie. Learn another language. Whatever you do, don't allow your thoughts to become bland. Diversify yourself. Add spice to your life. It doesn't matter where you come from, the right recipe can change your life forever. ▪

CHALLENGE

When you go to a buffet, try something you've never had before. But remember that diversity of thoughts is not just about food. It's adding a variety of mixtures and creative pieces that makes us unique. Just try it! You never know what you're missing.

EXERCISE

The last time I tried something new was_____

_____

My life is ☐ Spicy ☐ Bland.

Adding _____

_____

as a new experience can make my life more flavorful.

" The more we pour into someone else, the more room is made for us to receive additional information. It can reduce the time it takes for others to get where you are, and we have a lot of ground to cover. "

8

ONCE YOU LEARN...TEACH
PAY IT FORWARD

I love going to the park and seeing the tall water fountains. The water shoots out and splashes the kids standing beneath. For me it's a scene of joy and freedom. On a hot day, it's just what the doctor ordered. The kids are refreshed, the parents are smiling, and the world is a better place.

Now imagine what would happen if all that water spilled out onto the ground and evaporated. What would happen if the plumbing wasn't in place to recycle that water? All that fun would be reduced to a one-time event. The kids would go back to that same fountain and find no water there.

Just like fountains, as men we need our tanks refilled. But how do we do that? And why?

How? Look back and see who's coming along behind you, following in your footsteps, and spend time investing in them instead of stuff like cars, clothes, and money.

Why? The more we pour into someone else, the more room is made for us to receive additional information. It can reduce the time it takes for others to get where you are, and we have a lot of ground to cover.

We refill tanks by living so that others can be refreshed by the lessons of our successes and mistakes. We live so that others can be poured into. It would be a waste of refreshing ideas and experiences if we never shared them with anyone who could benefit from the knowledge. And in the same way, it would be a waste of a lifetime if you didn't teach others what you have learned.

We have to pour our experiences and wisdom into others throughout our journey. We can all teach someone else coming up behind us. We don't have to wait until we get degrees to be mentors. Whatever we learn, we can teach. We don't have to wait until we have that dream job with the dream salary, we can teach others right now!

You can be the 19-year-old pouring into the 9-year-old. Or you can be the 29-year-old pouring into the 19-year-old.

When you learn, teach. When you teach, learn. Pour into and invest in someone else. Once we read about it, we can write about it. No matter where we are in our journey, we can help others to get where we are going.

Remember as you help others, you are making room in your life for someone to help you! ▪

CHALLENGE

Make a decision to help one person a day.
Don't withhold experiences (good or bad) from others.
Teach someone else what you have learned so that
it takes them half the time to get what you have.

EXERCISE

How can you invest in someone's life
today?_____

_____took time
to pour into my life by _____
_____

I can help someone by sharing _____
_____
_____experience with them.

" Take time and give yourself an opportunity to be taught by your surroundings. The world is always giving us lessons, but are we learning from them?"

9

LIVE CURIOUSLY
CONTINUOUS LEARNING IN LIFE

When my daughter was a toddler, I learned so many things just by watching her every move. She was a very curious baby. Even at 12-13 months, I would catch her at the park looking at her surroundings. When she saw something new, she would instantly be attracted to it. If it were a leaf on a tree, or a squirrel, her eyes would lock in on the subject. She would touch the leaves, taste the leaves, and even pull on them until she was satisfied. Then, she'd move on to the next item. She would often ask the question most parents dread, "Why?" She would ask question after question until she had enough of an understanding, then move on to the next thing.

Imagine if we all approached our lives as young men this way. Curiously paying attention to the details. We could stop along the way to observe the smiles on people's faces, new flowers, or different sounds from the birds.

There's a popular verse in the Bible that says, "Be quick to listen and slow to speak." Whether you are familiar with the Bible or not, I think that's a good principal for life. I interpret this to mean: Don't approach something thinking you are so familiar with it that you can't learn from it.

Take time and give yourself an opportunity to be taught by your surroundings. The world is always giving us lessons, but are we learning from them? Take some time to ask yourself: Am I a continuous learner? What if I took some time to just observe more about my life? Do I slow down to observe? When was the last time I paid attention to the birds or the trees around me? What would I notice if I walked around my neighborhood and paid more attention to my neighbors? What might I discover if I actually paid attention?

The world can teach us something new today. But the only way we can learn it is if we develop a curiosity for it! ▪

CHALLENGE

Slow down and pay attention. Realize that you don't know it all. Understand that you haven't seen it all. Open up the door of your curiosity and be ready to learn something new!

EXERCISE

Am I a curious learner?   ☐ Yes ☐ No

Do I allow time to observe the small things in life?
☐ Yes ☐ No

66 Before you make a judgment,

you should strive for understanding.

...Critical friends aren't helpful;

understanding friends

last forever. 99

10

STRIVE FOR UNDERSTANDING
DON'T BE QUICK TO JUDGE

Growing up, I saw my mother struggle a lot. She worked countless hours trying to provide for my brothers and me. She was also involved in several unhealthy relationships. Some days, she was up, but most days, she was down.

We always had the necessities of life and never went without. I knew my mother always loved us, but I couldn't understand why she would deal with hurtful and unhealthy relationships. Why would she stay with guys who took her through heartbreak and disrespect? Why didn't she just leave? Besides, she was working and making a decent living, so in my mind, she didn't have to put up with any of it. Who would put up with abuse, misuse, and unhappiness? That was how I thought about it.

I later realized that she wasn't staying for herself... she was staying for us. She had three young boys and she wanted to provide us with the best life possible. Her love was filled with sacrifice. In exchange for the abuse and neglect, these men would provide financial stability. So she stayed, just to make sure that we kept a roof over our heads and clothes on our backs.

Before I understood my mother, I was critical. I judged her and made conclusions about her decisions for staying that weren't true. It wasn't until I was an adult with a family that I understood that sacrifices are necessary for your family. I also learned that as a child, details and circumstances aren't revealed.

I had to learn that before you make a judgment, you should strive for understanding. Don't be critical until you have full understanding. This can relate and apply to many different situations. Friends, parents, all conversations—make sure to get an understanding before you ruin friendships.

Critical friends aren't helpful; understanding friends last forever. ■

CHALLENGE

Take time to understand a person or a situation before you pass judgment. Ask before you criticize; listen before you talk. In all thy getting, get understanding.

EXERCISE

Is there a situation where you should have strived for understanding before passing judgment?

_____

_____

_____

_____

_____

_____

If so, when?

_____

_____

_____

_____

_____

_____

"I will not lose.

For even in defeat,

there's a valuable lesson learned,

so it evens up for me."

Jay-z, _Blueprint 2_

11

POOR VOICES LEAD TO POOR CHOICES
THE CLOSEST PEOPLE HAVE THE MOST INFLUENCE

Be careful who you let in your circle!

My older brother is two years older than me. As a younger brother, he was the one who I wanted to be like. He's always been the smart one. For him, intellect came easily. When we were kids, I was the one who had to work extra hard for the decent grade; he rarely had to study and would often get the best grade. He was naturally gifted and always artistic. He was so gifted that while in the 9th grade, he generated lots of interest from schools for his artistic ability and architectural design. But by the 11th grade, things began to change.

The faces and people in his life changed and began to have an impact on his decisions. He was the smart one, but he didn't know how to choose the right friends. Instead of applying himself in the classroom and academics, he was hanging out and cutting class. He went from fine tuning and progressing in his talents to neglecting them all together. In the end, his choice in friends became the main reason his life headed in a different direction. Even today, he hasn't lived up to a fraction of his potential simply because he allowed the pull of influence and peer pressure to override his natural abilities and talents.

We have to be selective with the people we allow in our lives. Yes, it may mean that you don't have all the cool friends at your house or that you might not be invited to the hottest parties. Remember if poor voices lead to poor choices, the opposite also holds true. Positive voices can lead to positive choices. So be careful who you allow to be your friend.

Ultimately, our closest friends will have the greatest influence in our lives. ■

CHALLENGE

Study your friends. Who is helping you to grow? Who are you allowing to hurt you by their influence in your life? How many friends work to make you better? How many friends are more of a distraction than they are a motivation? The more honest you are about your friends, the better you will be in the end.

EXERCISE

Make a list of people closest to you (Friends, cousins, brothers).

_____

_____

_____

_____

After you finish, list the ways that they influence you.

_____

_____

_____

_____

Also, list the ways that you influence their lives.

_____

_____

_____

_____

" I wanted to be an adult so badly

without realizing that I was discounting

the years that would prepare me to be a

responsible adult. I didn't realize that life

had a certain process that couldn't

be bypassed or expedited. "

12

WHAT'S THE RUSH?
THE PROCESS OF LIFE CAN'T BE EXPEDITED

My teenage years were much like a blur; I don't remember much. I had a habit of trying to expedite my youthful years and gravitating to interests that were beyond my age. I carried myself with the swag of an 18-year-old instead of the 15-year-old that I was. The guys I ran with were always a few years older than me and everything my older friends did, I wanted to do. On school nights, I worked until midnight not out of necessity, but because that's what my older friends did. I'd wish my days at school away not because I viewed learning as a waste of time, but because I didn't want to hang with the high school kids. Underage drinking and promiscuous sexual activity also accompanied my life as a teenager. One defining moment in my youth was my decision to skip my high school graduation and attend as a guest like the other adults instead of as a participant like my peers.

Why was I so anxious to rush those years away? Why was 'being grown' such a priority as a kid? Today I sit without many memories of being a kid. You know the types of stories that teenagers have when kids are kids? Wrestling, getting into mischief, and the simple joys of being a kid? Yeah, well... I don't have many of those. I don't remember after-school activities, clubs, lemonade sales, car washes, and races in the park.

Wasn't it interesting? I wanted to be an adult so badly without realizing that I was discounting the years that would prepare me to be a responsible adult. I didn't realize that life had a certain process that couldn't be bypassed or expedited. My experiences as a toddler were preparing me for the challenges I would face as a 10-year-old. My experiences as a teenager were preparing me for a young adulthood. Even my experiences as a young adult were preparing me for things to come later in life. Even though I was able physically to participate in underage drinking, premature sex, and a variety of other things that were beyond my years, I wasn't mentally or emotionally prepared. I later realized that I was trying to cheat at the process and not allow life to teach me the lessons necessary to move to the next stage of the process. ▪

CHALLENGE

Life is too short to rush through. Every once in a while, do something simple and age-appropriate. Shut down from the technology and take time to create unforgettable memories. When you feel pressure to be too old for your age, go out with friends who will make sure you have fun that is carefree, safe, and legal!

EXERCISE

What are some activities you enjoy?

_____

_____

_____

_____

How often do you make time for them?

_____

_____

_____

_____

"Many times the situation that felt uncomfortable was necessary to prepare me to one day look at another young man and help him navigate."

13

THE JOURNEY
TRANSITION CAN FEEL UNCOMFORTABLE

Every summer, my mother sent my brothers and me to vacation Bible school. Our church was a few blocks from our home, so we'd walk to this Sunday School-like program every day for an entire week. While there, we would hear stories from the Bible and we'd hang out with our friends. But the highlight of the day was the cookies and punch!

One day, as we walked home, we began to talk about one of the Biblical stories that stuck with us. The story was about Moses and his time in the wilderness. It turns out that Moses was removed from his homeland and brought to this "wilderness" place so he could be prepared for the Promised Land. I remember thinking, Why did God send him to such an uncomfortable place—to prepare him or teach a lesson? Why didn't he allow Moses to walk from his current place directly into the Promised Land? At that age, not many things made sense beyond the chocolate chip cookies and punch.

Fast forward into my early manhood years. During my journey, I remember the feeling of being in an uncomfortable span of time similar to "the wilderness."

Trying to navigate through life without the direction of a father or mentor would often leave me feeling isolated, alone, and frustrated.

Many times I felt like my life had no real purpose and I was "stuck in a rut"—both mentally and physically. I was moving forward, but had no sense of my true direction. I didn't know where I was going and I didn't have a map to help me get there. After years of frustration and several pity parties, I decided to look up and around. Right there in my life's rear-view mirror I began to understand the reasons behind some of the lessons. I realized that many times the situation that felt uncomfortable was necessary to prepare me to one day look at another young man and help him navigate. These moments of my life helped to build character. They helped me to become mentally tough and confident. Lastly, I realized that through the wilderness I had learned more about myself in isolation than I ever learned in community. ▪

CHALLENGE

Don't fight the isolation. Take time to enjoy the journey even if it means you will find yourself alone. Whatever it takes to get you to focus, do it and do it often. Take time to reflect. Take time to enjoy your life. In every chapter, remember that you are not at your final destination, so don't pressure yourself to place a period at the end of every sentence.

EXERCISE

List a time(s) when you felt isolated, alone, or "in the wilderness."

_____

_____

_____

_____

_____

" Every life will face challenges and disappointment. There is no human being on this earth who can say they have never had a bumpy day, or an unfortunate situation happen to them. So why do we act surprised? "

14

ENJOY THE RIDE
LESSONS FROM SCARS

My first time mountain biking was adventurous and painful. That day was filled with tough climbs up the hill, dangerous falls on the way down, and moments of pure exhilaration as I jumped over small ditches and creeks. The ride was bumpy and the bike was dirty, but should I have expected anything less? I wasn't going to the beach to lay out in the sun, I was going mountain biking!

The following day I was sore and stiff, but I had a blast! As a rider, there is no greater feeling than rushing adrenaline while reminiscing on the fun we had. During the ride, there were moments when I thought I would go over the cliff or hit a tree. It was scary, but something assured me that I would be all right.

My journey in life isn't much different than mountain biking. Sometimes filled with highs and lows, and by no means an easy, smooth, and bump-free journey. My life has had humps, bumps, and wrecks! I have news for you: Every life will face challenges and disappointment. There is no human being on this earth who can say they have never had a bumpy day, or an unfortunate situation happen to them. So why do we act surprised? When the painful days show up, why do we think, "Why is this happening to me?" Why do we hide in the dark shadows of our room, thinking the worst about ourselves? At what point will we realize—this is just a part of the ride?

The irony of the mountain biking experience is that I knew what to expect. I knew I would come home with scratches. I figured at some point I would fall. So, because I had clear expectations, I wasn't surprised by the toughness of the ride.

Note this: If you expect the bruises, you won't want to jump off the ride. If you expect the pain, you won't quit the moment pain shows up. The only way you can enjoy the ride is if you get a good grip on your expectations. Life has highs and lows, but if you expect both the high and the low, you won't be shocked when they hit. Enjoy the ride, guys! Bumps and bruises come with the territory. ▪

CHALLENGE

Challenge yourself by preparing your expectations for the celebrations and disappointments. When disappointments show up, don't bail out; you can recover. Don't jump off the ride just because life happened.

EXERCISE

List three times during the ride that you were disappointed.

_____

_____

_____

What could you have done differently to prepare yourself for what was to come?

_____

_____

_____

66 The difference between the man who changes and the child who stays the same is in his ability to tear down the walls. 99

15

WALLS
IT'S OK TO SHOW THE AUTHENTIC YOU

Isn't it amazing how carefree our lives are as toddlers? We are allowed to live without much of the worries and stresses of adulthood. There isn't much thought about the lack of money, new clothes, or the amount of food in the cabinet. During my time as a toddler, I got a free pass to just "be" my authentic self without thinking much about the nose I didn't like or how my teeth grew in after I lost a few. Somehow during my journey I lost the ability to just "be" and began listening to what others had to say or someone else's definition of who I should be.

As a child, my family didn't have many resources but we didn't realize it. We often wore "hand-me-downs" from the older kids in the family, and this was a normal instance throughout my childhood. Around 11 or 12 years old, in middle school, the teasing began. Kids would tease me because we couldn't afford a lot of new clothes, causing me to build walls.

"Walls" is a figure of speech describing my ability to hide or mask my lack of confidence. This was my way of keeping outsiders from getting close enough to discover the truth about our lack. I became an expert at building walls...walls of protection, walls of identity, walls of boundaries, walls of degree or vocation.

Once I left Detroit and realized there was a world beyond what I had experienced, my insecurities heightened. I thought surely no one would understand the dysfunction of my past. I felt like I had to put up more walls. I started hanging with lots of different kinds of people. My friends were now more diverse. But I wasn't used to this crowd. I didn't know how to articulate certain words and I lacked the vocabulary that these folks had because my friends didn't talk like that in Detroit! So I started to construct even more walls. I removed foul language and expanded my vocabulary. My plan worked for a little while, but one day, I realized: I am not being me! I had lost that ability from my childhood to just "be."

One of the first families I met when I moved south was the Chambless family. It was an instant connection! They would invite me over to their home during holidays or to watch a ball game. But because I walked into their home with walls around myself, I had a difficult time accepting any person who might not accept me for who I was. I wanted to keep them at arm's length in an effort to shield my true self.

After years of doing this, I realized that the same walls that were designed to keep others out were also keeping me in. The walls were not allowing me to just "be" my true self. In other words, what kept others out also kept me locked in. I was limiting myself from living a meaningful life all because I was afraid to show my friends the full me.

Whether your wall is a fear of reading or low self-esteem, it does not help to build what you cannot tear down. All of us have certain things that we wish we could change about ourselves. The difference between the man who changes and the child who stays the same is in his ability to tear down the walls. ■

CHALLENGE

Tell someone you trust about the walls in your life.
Why are they there? How did they get there? Why
are you afraid to be you? If you do not have any
walls, confront someone who does. Try to get them to
understand that you are their friend regardless of the
shame, guilt, or fear that he or she is holding onto. The
way forward is to tear down the walls, slowly but surely.

EXERCISE

I put up walls to hide _____

_____

I think people will think that I am _____
if they find out who I really am.

16

THESE SHOES ARE MEANT FOR YOU TO GROW INTO
RESPONSIBILITY COMES BEFORE UNDERSTANDING

When I was a child, money was tight. My mom would work several jobs at times in order to provide for us. One benefit of having three boys was the ability to pass clothes down to one kid after the older had outgrown them, better known as "hand-me-downs." One trick my mom used to get ahead of growth spurts was purchasing pants that were a few sizes too big. She would tuck the extra material underneath and press them until they looked true to size. As we grew, she would let the material out a half-inch at time. This allowed her to keep us in the same pants for an entire school year.

Eventually the multiple lines in the pants leg would give her secret away. My mom realized something: If she had given me the pants to wear on my own, I would have waited until they fit me before I put them on. She knew that although they were too big, one day I would grow into them.

The scenario that I experienced with clothes as a kid applies to my life and to the lives of many young men. The clothes represent the responsibilities that we face as fathers, husbands, sons, and friends. The idea of raising a child or providing for our families may seem as if it's too much for us to handle. For those of us without role models, self-doubt and insecurities quickly show up. For me, I looked at the responsibility with nervous anxiety, thinking, how could I possibly provide financial and emotional stability to this family? I was frightened at the magnitude of the responsibility.

Here's the beauty of life: We have time to grow into our responsibilities, similar to the way I had to grow into my pants as a kid. We won't have all of the answers today. We will make mistakes. But experience is part of the process of life. Everything we go through is meant to mature us. No one is born "ready" and "responsible." Responsibility is a learned behavior. In other words, we learn it over time. We make mistakes that grow us. We pay attention to the success and challenges of other people around us and learn from them. To be responsible means that we learn, over time, to take ownership of our actions. This also means understanding what we lack and reaching out to potential mentors to learn from. ■

CHALLENGE

Give yourself space to grow. Don't beat yourself up when you make a mistake. If you mess up, study your error and try to avoid it the next time. Put yourself around friends who will help you and not hurt you. If you do, you will have a support system to keep you accountable whenever you lose focus.

EXERCISE

Doing _____
seems like something I would never be able to do.

I think _____ is an amazing person.

He/she can do _____
and I can see myself doing that one day.

_____ has stopped me from
pursuing the type of life that I want.

" When you discover your roots,

you discover parts of yourself.

You uncover mysteries. You have the

knowledge from generations

that came before you. **"**

17

A TREE WITHOUT ROOTS
WHO ARE YOU?

A few years ago, I was having Thanksgiving dinner with a good friend. This was your traditional Thanksgiving meal where several families drive for hours to celebrate with each other. The smell of turkey and dressing was in the air and a football game was on the TV. I remember grandparents, aunts, and uncles congregating in the kitchen to catch up on the latest pictures and events surrounding the kids. I saw a grandson talking to his grandfather. The grandfather told stories about his grandparents. He was sharing a recipe that was passed down from his grandfather.

I remember thinking to myself, "Wow! This is how it works."

Granddads pass down information about the legacy of their family to their grandchildren. Parents offer vivid memories of cousins, aunts, and uncles. At family reunions, children learn about their family heritage. Family secrets and traditions are passed down, giving the younger generations a glimpse of the past.

Problem is, I didn't have that advantage. I was born like a tree without roots.

Outside of my father, I don't know any of my relatives. I didn't have a strong relationship with my father—the only person around in my family—so that left me, a lot of times, scratching my head. I never met my grandparents and I surely don't know my great-grandparents. So that means I didn't have the type of information being passed down at this Thanksgiving gathering. I don't know where a lot of my built-in traits and tendencies come from.

As I grew into a young man, I remember thinking, I wonder if I have my grandfather's nose or, I wonder if my tendencies are genetic. Who am I?!

Every young person should be connected to their heritage. If we don't know where we come from, we start life with several question marks. We don't know if the things we bring to the table, whether positive or negative, are a result of our DNA or not. We could be fighting hard against something that is simply born in us through our family line. But for many of us, we don't have the privilege of knowing our past.

African Americans in particular struggle around this issue. Many of us do not know where we come from because our lineage was broken apart during slavery. Like trees without roots, we live in spaces with no definition.

How can someone name an oak tree if that tree doesn't have roots? When a tree doesn't know its roots, it will always guess its way through life: Am I an apple tree? Am I an orange tree? What kind of tree am I?

Discovering your heritage can be as important as the education you will receive throughout your life. When you discover your roots, you discover parts of yourself. You uncover mysteries. You have the knowledge from generations that came before you. ▪

CHALLENGE

As you grow, work on identifying your roots. If possible, talk to your family about your history. Make it a priority to discover who you are. The older you get, the more you'll realize just how important these conversations are.

EXERCISE

My actions mostly resemble _____ in my family.

I'm most proud of _____ ___ habit that was passed down in my family.

I can trace my lineage back to _____ generations.

"We should never live life in the

shadows of somebody else's opinion.

We should never let a gang tell us who

we are. We should live in confidence, in

appreciation, and in satisfaction of who

God made us.**"**

18

WHO AM I?
SELF-DISCOVERY

What is the true purpose of a mirror? Mirrors reflect or represent an image. When we stand in front of a mirror, it reflects an exact image of our exterior. Our actions, on the other hand, reflect who we are on the inside, our hearts and minds.

Life is like a mirror. In order to see what we look like, we've got to be willing to confront the reflection. I had a huge self-discovery phase and my path was not simple. The route I had to take was a long one.

Throughout my life, I had certain traits and characteristics that were positive and some were negative, but I never took time to understand them. I would often find myself only giving 50% in relationships while keeping the remaining 50% close and what I perceived to be safe. I would enter into relationships—intimate, amicable. or buddy-buddy—feeling as if I couldn't trust a person 100%. I questioned why those people were in my life and what they truly wanted.

After years of failed or surface level relationships, I had to look in the mirror and ask who I was and why I behaved this way. I had to step up to the mirror and look at all the things that made me, me. I realized that not only was I unwilling to trust, but I also came to understand why. Once I was honest with myself, I realized that I had been let down so many times by my father as a child that I was reserved about trusting others.

When I was a child, my mother and father divorced and my court-mandated time with my father was limited to every other weekend. I looked forward to spending time with my father. At seven or eight years old, I would wake up on Saturday mornings with excitement. I would dress myself, pour cereal and milk, then wait. My brothers were often watching Saturday morning cartoons, but not me. I would sit on the sofa by the window and wait.

Many times I would wait the entire day with no word from my father. He would often call the following day with an excuse for the day before. Over time, I stopped listening to the excuses. I stopped waiting. I started to think, If my father would leave me hanging, there's no telling what a stranger would do. From that point on, I began to build a defense mechanism, a trait to keep myself protected from the hurt of disappointment.

Has this defense mechanism worked? Of course not. All it really accomplished was to keep me from having true relationships. But I would not have discovered this about myself had I not looked in the mirror and asked, "Who am I, and why do I do what I do?"

We can't grow as people until we find out who we are and why we do the things we do. Our behaviors and habits mold us, but they also tell us about the areas in our lives that need to grow. When we know who we are, we realize the WHY behind all of our actions. We realize why we like certain things and despise other things. If we know the details behind our shyness, then we don't have to change what is natural about ourselves. If we know the why behind our risk-taking personalities, then we don't need to apologize for being ourselves.

The worst person is the person who becomes whatever their current environment tells them to be. So, if they're in one group, they act a certain way, but if they're around another crowd, they behave according to that crowd's expectations. They allow others to dictate their behavior instead of being themself.

Sure there will be things we don't like. And there may be things that we do like. But whatever the case, we should never live life in the shadows of somebody else's opinion. We should never let a gang tell us who we are. We should live in confidence, in appreciation, and in satisfaction of who God made us.

Asking the question, "Who am I" isn't a one-time conversation. The answer will always lead to more questions, like, "What are my passions?" "What are my weaknesses?" and "Who are my mentors?"

If we are dishonest about who we are, we can't be honest about who we are not. Knowing who we are will secure us as people, and will help us to decide who we will NOT be. ■

CHALLENGE

Stand in the mirror and answer the hard questions, like, "What am I afraid of? What if I don't live up to the expectations of my family? Who do I most resent in my family? Who am I most proud of?" Take time by yourself to learn about yourself.

Dedicate a Saturday morning or a few days to think deep and hard about these questions. What makes you tick? What makes you smile? Why do you do what you do?

EXERCISE

If I were to receive an award, what would I want that award to be for?

_____

_____

_____

_____

_____

Beginning when I was a child, what are the five most significant events in my life?

_____

_____

_____

_____

19

EFFORT + TALENT = PROGRESS
TALENT ISN'T ENOUGH

Detroit is known to be a breeding ground for high-quality basketball players. Street ball is often a rite of passage into teenage years or simply gaining credibility in your neighborhood. When I grew up, some of the guys in my neighborhood could really play ball. These were the 6'10" guys with great, natural gifts for winning state championships. Ironically, not many made it to the college or professional level. Why is that? Surely they had the physical talent to excel at the game. Some of them were hard-working young men. But many of them didn't have the mental dedication to go to the gym or practice on a regular basis. Instead, they relied on natural talent. As a result, they didn't develop their gifts. It wasn't because they weren't good; it was because they didn't put any effort into their craft.

There were also the guys who were, by some accounts, too short, or too slow or lacked many of the natural qualities of the blue chip guys. But they did have qualities that the others didn't. They had a natural drive that made up for their lack of height. They were the first to arrive at practice, ate the right food, studied hard and stayed out of trouble. Many of them were model athletes and had qualities that would carry them beyond basketball.

Our lives become amazing when we find that balance between effort and purpose, when we understand what our God-given talents are and work to develop and improve them. This is the point where our mental and physical strengths are working together. The moment these lines intersect, you will see progress!

Notice: I didn't say that you will see success. Why? Because success means different things to different people. Progress, on the other hand, is constant movement forward. When we're making progress, we don't stop at one award or one promotion. We make a steady decision to match effort with purpose.

Listen: True talent doesn't feel like work, it feels like fulfillment. We walk away every day realizing, "This is what I was created to do."

What are your talents? Where is your effort? You show me a person who has effort and is developing his talents, and I'll show you a man who is making progress.

Just because you are good, that should never stop you from striving for great! The process of constant improvement never ends. We will always have something we can do better no matter how talented we are. The moment we assume that we have crossed the finished line is the moment our progress slows or stops. ■

CHALLENGE

What are you doing with your life? How are your hours spent during the day? Are you wasting time watching more television and playing video games? Will this benefit you in the end? While in school, which subjects make you pay attention? Which classes are most intriguing? Maybe the subject you love most is the place where your purpose is hiding.

EXERCISE

_____ is easy for me to do, but I'm not motivated to get it done.

_____ is difficult for me to do, but I can see myself doing it to make a difference in my life or in the life of someone else.

" Your purpose must align

with your efforts.

What are you waiting for?

Start the discovery process

right now! "

$$\boxed{20}$$

DISCOVERING YOUR PURPOSE
INVEST YOUR TIME WHERE YOU GET ENERGY

If money weren't an issue, what would you do? How would you live? Where would you serve?

When I was younger, I had a passion for making a difference. My goal was taking time to help other people. Sometimes it was shoveling an elderly neighbor's snow or helping my grandmother put up groceries. My satisfaction came from helping others.

My true love was teaching. I always had time to help a young person with their academic journey. When it was time to choose a profession, however, teaching fell off the list. How did this happen? I was young and focused on the lifestyle that I wanted to afford. I decided to go in another direction: I crawled into the world of finance. It didn't take me long to realize, "I can get good at this craft, but I'm empty." It didn't fulfill me.

I was making a decent salary and providing for my family, but I wasn't satisfied. So every day I went home empty. That is, until I started volunteering in the classrooms of high schools and universities.

Even though my academic training was focused in one area, my purpose was to teach and make an impact. By putting energy into my purpose, I received a breath of fresh air. I felt better and more energetic.

Discovering your purpose is the best gift you can ever give yourself. Your purpose is not a job; it is a calling. It's something you were born to do for the world. Remember, I loved to teach, but I didn't necessarily have to be in a classroom to do it. This book, for example, is another way that I am flexing my teaching muscles. All I knew was that I wanted to make an impact. I wanted to shine light onto someone else so that they could learn from my journey. Whether I was behind a podium or in front of a desk didn't matter. I just wanted to help others to see life differently.

The point is simple: Your purpose must align with your efforts. What are you waiting for? Start the discovery process right now! Don't waste your time or energy studying a field that you really don't care about. When you look back through the years of your life, I hope you won't regret the things you've placed your energy into. What is your purpose? If someone asked you to define it, what would you say? What are you doing to water the plant of purpose? If your plant dies, your zeal for life dies. Your energy will die. Your hope will dwindle away. ▪

CHALLENGE

Find the link between your passion and serving people. All purpose is linked to people. Whatever drives you will help to escort someone else. What is that "thing" for you? Perhaps you love working in homeless shelters, because you are called to help end poverty. Maybe you want to work as a banker, because you have been purposed to make an impact on global finances or to help young families build financial futures or their own homes. Follow the push. Follow the pull. The answer to discovering your purpose is closer than you think.

EXERCISE

I would do _____ despite the money that I would make.

If I could do _____, it would make my life complete.

Our purpose often involves another person. I can see this when I do _____.

■

"As men we were taught to hold it in.

That's why we don't know how 'til

we're older men."

Common, *Love Is*

■

21

COMMUNICATION
THE BENEFITS OF EXPRESSING YOURSELF

In my family we had 13 cousins, seven guys and six girls. We would spend what felt like every waking moment together. We would spend the night at each other's homes, forming huge pallets on the floor with blankets, pillows, and whatever else we could find to keep us both warm and comfortable. Life seemed to have no worries when we were together. No matter where the location, the scene was the same.

The girls would immediately congregate in one section of the house and begin to talk, or as we put it, "the chatter would begin." The guys would huddle around the television or toss a football. No matter what the activity, the outcome was the same. If an issue or disagreement arose we would push, shove, or fight. An hour later we would be back to normal.

I've often wondered how men can communicate by saying so few words. We can watch a two-hour basketball game and only say ten words to each other and not have a problem. As a young man, I was taught to suppress my thoughts and feelings, often being told to "stop being a little girl" and "suck it up."

Communication, or the expression of thoughts and

feelings, is an important part of my make-up but it was suppressed as a young person. Being forced to suppress feelings and emotions is kind of like a balloon filled with air. This, my young brothers, is the worst thing you can ever do.

I'm sure you've seen the consequences of a balloon with too much air. At first, it expands larger and larger. But eventually, the balloon pops because it has to find a release. In other words, taking in the stresses of life without an outlet can cause you to pop. It can cause me to pop as well.

Communication and the expression of emotions aren't seen as "manly." But I would encourage you to practice the ideal of expressing yourself in a meaningful and constructive way. This can include both verbal and written communication. It may not come naturally to you, and I understand. But if you're going to grow as a man, you've got to work at communicating with others. ▪

CHALLENGE

Start a conversation with a man you know. Maybe he's your dad, uncle, or neighbor. Find out how things have changed or stayed the same since he was your age.

EXERCISE

Ask these questions to a man you know and trust:

Are things different for me than when you were growing up?

_____

Is anything the same?

_____

Has technology changed you for the better?

_____

Why or why not?

_____

_____

Which famous people did you admire?

_____

Did you ever get lonely as a kid?

_____

" All habits aren't bad habits.

...Here's the message:

Intentionally choose to create

habits that will benefit you. "

22

CREATING GOOD HABITS
BEING INTENTIONAL

My job in the military was as a cook. We would feed one or two thousand troops per meal, seven days a week. Often I worked the morning shift; our start time was 3:30 am. At this point in my life, I was nineteen years old and loved to hang out, so most mornings I would show up to work after two to three hours of sleep. Coffee quickly became my best friend. Each morning would begin with one cup immediately then another after an hour or so. Before I knew it, I was drinking four or five cups of coffee per shift. Many times I had the same routine even if I'd had enough sleep. An action that began with one cup as needed became a habit of consuming coffee whether I needed it or not.

Without thinking, I was making daily decisions that could have had an effect on my health. I was acting out of habit. We create habits when we do something over and over again. I once read, "When habits emerge, the brain stops participating in decision making." In other words, once we learn something, our brain goes into autopilot mode. Subconsciously, habits often guide our behavior. They help us maneuver through our lives without much thought or intent.

All habits aren't bad habits though. Think about the kid who creates a habit of studying every day before he picks up the Xbox. How about the kid who jogs a mile before school? Whatever habit you are trying to form or is currently in existence should include the following questions: What results I am shooting for? Am I achieving those results? Am I an expression of my best self when I do this? Here's the message: Intentionally choose to create habits that will benefit you. ▪

CHALLENGE

Take time to evaluate your actions. Are you going through life on auto pilot? Or do your actions have a purpose? Choose to intentionally create good habits.

EXERCISE

Choose one bad habit that you would like to break. What is the habit?

_____

_____

By what date would you like to break this habit?

_____

_____

What's your plan of attack?

_____

_____

How will you reward yourself after you succeed?

_____

_____

" When you allow people to see

who you are day in and day out,

you have begun the journey toward

consistency. Consistency allows

those watching us to understand

who we are at the core. "

23

CONSISTENCY
WHO ARE YOU AT THE CORE?

When I was in the army, we did physical training every day. We would often run three to five miles with 100 to 200 push-ups and sit-ups each day. I had friends who looked like they were body builders. We would weigh in with our shirts off and the competitive side of me would compare all our "manly" muscles... biceps, chest, and shoulders. I would think to myself, What are we doing differently? We run every day together, we do push-ups and sit-ups together, we practically eat the same things. How are our bodies so drastically different?

Sometimes I would do a few extra push-ups in an effort to gain on them, but then I was back to eating and drinking unhealthy foods. I didn't sustain the behavior over time. What I didn't realize was that each day after each workout the more muscular guys would go to the gym and put in more work. In addition to eating foods that were healthy, they were resting their bodies and drinking plenty of fluids. Each day, they repeated the same behavior when no one was watching, creating patterns that were beneficial.

I learned a valuable lesson: What you do when no

one's looking helps you create consistent behavior. These guys consistently ate the right foods. They consistently worked out. They were consistently resting their bodies. It wasn't about what they were doing when we worked out together. It was their consistency that allowed them to have better bodies than the rest of us who worked out with them.

By definition, consistency means the steadfast adherence to the same principles. My translation of this is: When your words match your actions over time. So, if you consistently go to the gym, then your muscles will eventually grow. If you read the newspaper everyday, then your vocabulary will expand. What you think about inside will manifest on the outside.

When you allow people to see who you are day in and day out, you have begun the journey toward consistency. Consistency allows those watching us to understand who we are at the core. Our consistency (or lack thereof) will show others how respectful, arrogant, generous, selfish, or caring we are. Consistency allows others to know how much they can depend on us, how much they can trust us, what our boundaries are, and what they can expect from us. At every stage in our lives, people will want to know where we stand, what our moral values are, and how well we walk the walk. ■

CHALLENGE

Consistency isn't about doing something one time; it's doing something with the same level of quality over time. What do your actions over time say about you?

EXERCISE

Think about actions that are consistent in your life. What are they?

_____

_____

What does it say about you to others?

_____

_____

" Responsible men will know

how to respond to any situation.

We set structure,

and we set an example.

If we fail to do that, we fail to be

responsible men. "

24

RESPONSIBILITY
WE HAVE TO STEP IT UP

My mom is a hard-working 25-year veteran of the prison system. She provided for her three boys by dedicating countless hours to working with criminals. When I was of age she would allow me to use her car while she was working. I would pull up to the prison where she worked, let her out, and watch her walk through heavily guarded gates.

Once I arrived a little early and decided to go inside the lobby and wait. It was a surprise realizing that the workers were just as locked in as the prisoners were. I asked my mom how it felt to go to work in a prison and lock herself up with criminals every day. She replied, "If the men in this prison understood their responsibilities in life, I would be out of a job."

Those words didn't mean much to me until I grew into a man and began to understand the roles and responsibilities of manhood. By studying men who I looked up to, I discovered my true responsibility as a man. I discovered that it's our responsibility to create structure in our homes, build confidence in our children, and uplift and honor our wives. It's also the responsibility of men to reduce chaos in our communities.

If we are adding to the chaos and ruining the structure, we are not taking responsibility for our lives. We have to be sure that if we bring children into the world, we are able to provide for them. We can't blame the system or live off of others for the rest of our lives.

We've got to take responsibility now. If we failed the test, we don't blame the teacher. We take responsibility and decide to study harder. If we crashed the car because we were texting, we need to be honest with ourselves. We don't blame the innocent person involved. We take responsibility for what we did.

Nowadays, society has decided that those who make the most money are the people responsible for raising our community. That means, if women make more money than men, we will hand over the responsibility to the women. But this isn't the way it should go. Responsibility has little to do with money, and has all to do with ownership. Our job is to create structure in our families regardless of how much money we make.

Responsible men will know how to respond to any situation. We set structure, and we set an example. If we fail to do that, we fail to be responsible men. ■

CHALLENGE

Someday all of us will have the opportunity to lead families, our communities, or a group of coworkers. They are not expecting a mistake-free leader, they are looking for a responsible leader. Are you willing to step up and be responsible?

EXERCISE

I define being responsible as_____
_____

I consider irresponsibility to be_____
_____

It's easier for me to blame someone.
☐ Yes ☐ No

I'm the kind of person who owns his actions.
☐ Yes ☐ No

66 In life, we will face challenges

that feel like a roller coaster ride.

Don't get off the coaster. **99**

25

FAILURE ISN'T FAILURE UNTIL YOU QUIT
QUITTING CAN'T BE A PART OF THE PLAN

I was an extremely curious kid and took pride in understanding how things work together. I would often wonder with great amazement at how technology worked. How a cassette and CD could store music or how a smoke detector actually detected smoke.

For Christmas, I would ask for an electronic item like a radio simply to explore. So less than a few hours after receiving the radio I would go to my mother's basement and disassemble the radio in its entirety. Transmitters, circuit boards and all would lay on the basement floor with one goal in mind: To understand how the parts worked together and to reassemble each piece in its original working condition. As I disassembled more complex items, like my mom's blender, often I would have five or so screws left over. I would often try for hours disassembling and reassembling the item without understanding where I went wrong. I had a choice; I could quit and hope the blender would work without them or keep trying until I got it right. I chose to keep trying.

Life can often resemble my need to discover what's behind the molded plastic casing of a radio, blender, or smoke detector. Our curiosity allows us to wander into situations without understanding how to put things back together.

We all will face difficulties that allow us to feel like failures. But the failure is only a failure if we give up and quit. Take a person who has a hard time with math. A low score on a test can make anyone feel defeated. But the low score doesn't make him a failure. He must have the desire to continue to study, taking the small wins like a D, improving to a C-, and eventually to a B.

In life, we will face challenges that feel like a roller coaster ride. Don't get off the coaster. Don't quit; stick with it. For every downhill drop, twist, turn, and giant loop, the roller coaster almost always lets you off safely. ▪

CHALLENGE

Life will often throw things our way that will challenge us. The challenging issue isn't what defines us, it's how we respond. How will you respond?

EXERCISE

What have you tried lately and quit? Why did you quit?

_____

_____

How long did you try before you gave up?

_____

_____

What lesson did you learn that you can use some other time?

_____

_____

What would you do differently if given another opportunity?

_____

_____

"Preparation for an opportunity begins well before it seems necessary.

Our preparation, along with our persistence, gives us an opportunity to practice and fail without any repercussions."

26

HEAT EXHAUSTION
WHAT HAPPENS IF WE DON'T PREPARE

Summers in Detroit are often hot and humid. Temperatures often exceed 90-plus degrees, with 100% humidity from the Great Lakes.

When I was in the seventh grade, me and a few friends decided we would try out for the neighborhood football team. We played basketball at the park or in someone's back yard during the summer and often took breaks when it was too hot, but football tryouts were slightly different. The day before tryouts, my mom told me to drink lots of water, because of the weather forecast. She told me very clearly not to drink soft drinks instead of water.

Like many 12-year-olds, I thought I knew more than my mom. So I decided to enjoy my Faygo fruit punch drink on the day of tryouts instead of water. The first ten minutes of practice went as expected—pushups, running, and more pushups. The next 45 minutes, however, felt like torture, the sun beating on my skin and my half-full water container was now empty. As my mouth dried and my legs cramped, I heard my mother's words clearly: "Prepare for the worst, because it's going to get hot."

As I have lived my life, I've realized that my mother's words apply to more than football practice. Preparation for an opportunity begins well before it seems necessary. Our preparation, along with our persistence, gives us an opportunity to practice and fail without any repercussions. Preparation could be studying for a test, practicing for an audition, or learning how to present effectively in front of an audience. Whatever the occasion, remember not to wait until you get to the practice field to hydrate. Plan ahead and avoid losing a spot on the team due to leg cramps and exhaustion. ■

CHALLENGE

You don't know when you'll be required to perform and you wont always get a second chance. Are you a "live in the moment" person scrambling to prepare once you get a chance? I challenge you to stay ready; this way you will never have to get ready.

EXERCISE

My dream opportunity is to _____

_____

_____

_____

_____

_____

I am doing _____

_____

_____to prepare for my big opportunity.

" Let your passion, persistence and preparation chart your path! Your new path may feel lonely; it's O.K., it's a new path. That's what's going to allow you to live your life beyond others' expectations. "

27

LIFE BEYOND EVERYONE'S EXPECTATIONS
CHART YOUR OWN PATH

As a young person, I was average at many things. I was a C+, B- student. On the court, I had average ball-handling skills and a mediocre jump shot. I could run, but not fast enough to make the track team. My life, in others' eyes, was average, so their expectations of me were average.

I wasn't motivated to try new things. After all, I was deemed an average kid who would live an average life. Hearing my siblings praised for their potential or being motivated to explore all possibilities for their lives created a chip on my shoulder and a little animosity toward them.

The truth is that those who considered me average didn't account for my ambition, my love of learning, and my curiosity to understand how things worked together. I later understood that people often set expectations on your life based on their own journey and position in life.

Many times we solicit input from family members and people we trust and this often becomes the blueprint of our journey. But people can only advise you based on their own journey. It can be tough for a parent to feel comfortable advising you to go someplace they have never been. Yet if someone recommends that we take a certain path, without question we head off down that path.

Let your passion, persistence and preparation chart your path! Your new path may feel lonely; it's O.K., it's a new path. That's what's going to allow you to live your life beyond others' expectations. ∎

Challenge

Those people closest to you will often attempt to define your life based on their definitions of success. Will you chart your own path, follow your own dreams, or let someone else define your future?

Exercise

I love to do_____
and no one knows about it.

If I could define my future, I would make _____
_____ impact on the world.

" Take a new path,

try a new book, or try something

that you never experienced.

...Try a new something

and surprise yourself. **"**

28

SURPRISE YOURSELF
FOCUS ON THE FUTURE

Have you ever done something and looked back and said, "Wow, I didn't know I had that in me?"

When I served in the military, we would often conduct training exercises that I would not have explored on my own. One of my assignments sent me to Northern California with a light infantry battalion. Once a year, we would hike 17 miles in full gear with a 50-pound backpack. Growing up in a city with plenty of public transportation, there was never a desire or necessity to walk 17 miles. Nor did I think there was a reason to jump out of a perfectly good plane or spend 90 days in the desert.

We often have untapped potential that is waiting to be awakened. The awakening can come from new exposure, new adventures, or simply dreaming a new dream. As humans, we often choose the paths that are most comfortable and that result in a familiar setting.

Take a new path, try a new book, or try something that you never experienced. You may find something new about yourself, a new strength, a new like and dislike. Try a new something and surprise yourself. ∎

CHALLENGE

The surprise will come from you. Do you have it in you to take the step outside of what you know?

EXERCISE

_____
_____is something that
I've always wanted to try but haven't.

I will try a new _____
before the week is over.

I was surprised when I tried _____.
The result was_____.

29

THE ROAD NEVER ENDS
THE JOURNEY IS LIFELONG

I remember taking my first road trip in my own car. It was a 1987 Ford Escort hatchback with no A/C. But it was my gateway to freedom. It allowed me to drive to school, my job, and simply to hang out with the neighborhood guys.

My first solo trip was for my high school senior picnic. We were to meet at the beach of Lake St. Clair Shores, which is typically an hour drive from Detroit. This was 1991. The only people using GPS units worked for the government. Internet searches and Google maps were yet to be invented, so my only modes for directions were a map, which I didn't own, or word of mouth.

I proceeded on my journey with directions from another student. About 30 minutes into the trip I realized I only had the name of the 50-mile lake. I hadn't asked for specific directions to the location of the cookout. I drove another 10 minutes before pulling over and gathering myself for a game plan. With just enough gas in my car to make a round trip journey to and from the lake, I realized I didn't have room for error. I turned around and headed back to Detroit.

The next day, classmates told me there were directions posted on a sign as you exited the freeway, pointing us to the correct location.

Often times this happens to us in life. We begin a journey and are uncertain of where the road ends or which direction we should go. Had I driven an additional 10 minutes I would have realized that my situation wasn't as daunting as it seemed; after all I had completed 80% of my journey. But I let fear of the unknown deter me from finishing the trip.

Finish the trip. We won't always know when and where the road will end, but if we are passionate and have prepared for the moment, our fears can be used as fuel to propel us to complete the journey. ■

CHALLENGE

Life is often uncertain. During your journey you will be faced with situations that are unclear or uncertain. Will you accept the challenge and finish the journey?

EXERCISE

Are you afraid of what's ahead? ☐ Yes ☐ No

If so, what will you do to overcome your fears?

_____

_____

_____

❝ Because many young men lack positive images and role models, they also lack the ability to communicate, lead their families, and become who they were designed to be. ❞

30

IF ONLY YOU KNEW
INSECURITIES: WE ALL HAVE THEM. NOW WHAT?

What are insecurities?

If you're good at shooting free throws, it's because you spent endless hours practicing. You didn't wake up one day and know how to make a perfect shot. You had to practice until one day you became good. Now that you're good, there is no pressure when game time comes. Your practice and familiarity with the game has given you the confidence and the security to step up.

But imagine if you had to shoot the winning putt during a round of golf. You've never picked up a club, you've never been to a golf range, and you are totally unfamiliar with this particular game. The goal is the same—get the ball into the hole—but there are different rules and a different field. So, you might not feel as confident to hit the ball.

Welcome, brothers, to the world of insecurity!

Insecure people lack confidence. They lack the trust in themselves to perform certain tasks. Growing up, one of my biggest insecurities came from the absence of a positive male role model. I was a young man growing up in inner-city Detroit with no direction or purpose. Chaos and reckless living surrounded me. Eventually, I got used to that kind of lifestyle. There were no rules and few expectations for my life. I kind of made up my own rules as I went along.

But one day...I became a man. At least, that's what my age told me. I didn't know what that meant. What was I supposed to do differently? How should I interact with family and friends? Did my age really define my manhood? I had a real insecurity. I didn't know how to be a man!

I didn't have a reference point for what a real man looked like. So I accepted false images from movies, neighborhood superstars, and other influences regarding what a man should or should not do. Eventually I lost confidence. I didn't have a roadmap.

The truth is, we all have insecurities. We all have things from our upbringing, environment, or families that we attempt to hide even from those closest to us. Because many young men lack positive images and role models, they also lack the ability to communicate, lead their families, and become who they were designed to be. The result is a lackluster life, failed relationships, and continual cycles of failure. ■

CHALLENGE

Understand and embrace your insecurities. Find a positive image from a coach, teacher, or a relative to use as a guide—somebody living, breathing, and close by in case you need to reach out for information. When you find that positive image, learn from them by paying attention. You will learn how to respect women, your elders, and even yourself.

EXERCISE

Choose 3 words to describe your strengths.

_____

_____

_____

Choose 3 words to describe your insecurities.

_____

_____

_____

" No matter if you are the sun

or the moon, we all have bright gifts

and talents. We were all created

as individuals to shine. "

31

NEVER DIM YOUR OWN LIGHT
DON'T WAVER ON YOUR PRINCIPALS

It's a normal Saturday morning. You grab a bowl of cereal and walk to the window to enjoy the beautiful sunshine. But today is different from any other Saturday. Today, the light appears to be dull. The clouds are blocking the light. Everything seems so sad and gloomy. You wake up the next day and realize the sun hasn't come out yet again. The same thing happens for a few more days, and days turn into weeks. Weeks turn into months. News reporters tell of devastation in the land. The crops have gone bad, animals are getting sick, and humans have become depressed!

The meteorologist finally discovers the sad news. It turns out, the sun decided not to shine his light because his buddy, the moon, was jealous of his ability to light up the earth. The moon became upset because he only got to shine at night, and he felt like no one paid him much attention. Everyone was asleep by the time his light shined in the world.

Not realizing how important his role was (especially to the ocean and wildlife), the sun retired from shining. He was so busy trying to make the moon happy that he forgot his purpose.

No matter if you are the sun or the moon, we all have bright gifts and talents. We were all created as individuals to shine. Along this journey, I have learned how dangerous it is to compare myself to others. Your talents are not my talents; my accomplishments are not your accomplishments.

Our success may look different, but as long as we both shine, the world is a better place. As you grow into manhood, don't dim your light. Don't reduce your worth because others around you aren't as "bright" as you are. Don't settle for the norm, when you are created for excellence.

The moment you dim your light is the moment the world will cease to shine as brightly as it once did. It becomes a little darker than times past. Resist this desire as often as possible. Today is your day to shine. Your true love, your true friends, and your true family members are not in competition with you. True relationships will last. True relationships will always empower you to grow because of someone else's light. Refuse today to dim yourself for anyone else—no matter who they are. ■

CHALLENGE

Are you the sun or the moon in this chapter? If you are
the sun, keep shining. If you are the moon, don't be
discouraged. Your role is just as important as anyone else's.

EXERCISE

I downplayed knowing _____
because I knew it would make my friends uncomfortable.

I respect_____
for being who they are everyday.

" If you fall, then make it

worth the ride.

...The fall won't destroy you.

The main purpose of it

is to build you. "

32

IF YOU DON'T FALL,
YOU NEVER LEARN

When babies first learn to walk, they have to take various steps before they master the art of walking. Usually, babies start out by crawling. They crawl from one side of the room to the other. Then, they learn how to stand in one place on their own two feet. While doing this, they learn how to strengthen their legs and build their muscles. After that, they grab on to a coffee table and skirt the edge of the table by taking small steps. Finally, when they have practiced long enough, they will move away from the training wheels of a table and try to walk across the room on their own.

We all know what happens at first—they fall! They tumble to the ground and they have to get up and try again. It would be an amazing miracle if any baby who ever tried walking never ever fell at least once before mastering it.

We can't be afraid of the fall. Everyone falls at some point in life. There is not one human being that has no record of falling. But the falls help us to learn. The falls help us to strengthen our muscles and try different techniques. Our falls lift us. Most importantly, it's our falls that lift someone else.

So don't be afraid to move forward. Your success is on the other side of the fall. Our falls keep us grounded. Our falls make us human.

Many young brothers are afraid to fall. So guess what they do? Nothing. They never let go of the coffee table because they don't want anybody laughing at them if they fall in public. Fear of failure keeps them locked down and unproductive.

If you fall, then make it worth the ride. Nobody wants to fall, but everybody has done it. So obviously, the fall won't destroy you. The main purpose of it is to build you. ■

CHALLENGE

Think about the props you have used to hold you up. Are you holding onto your parents, friends, or family members? Who or what do you need to let go of so that you can learn to walk on your own? When you conquer your fear of falling, you will eventually learn to fly.

EXERCISE

In the past 12 months I have learned_____ from trying and failing.

_____

_____ hurt when I fell, but this is the lesson I learned_____.

" Every day you should water

the garden of your goals.

Until you focus on your future,

your future will not

focus on you. "

33

THE GOAL SETTER
DECIDE WHERE YOU WANT TO GO BEFORE YOU GO THERE

If I asked you to list your twelve-month goals, your three-year goals, and your five-year goals, what would they be? Are you trying to save money? Do you plan to graduate on time? Do you want to get married? What are the things you want to see change in your life?

In all things, we have to be realistic. Your goal may be to become a millionaire in five years, but how do you plan to do that? What are you doing to make that happen? Where are you working? Are you interning for a major corporation? I'm sure everyone wants to have a big house and become a great legend in the world, but do you think that will happen playing video games all day?

The most important reason for establishing goals is so that we can track our progress. If you have ever been to a track meet, you know that coaches have practiced with these athletes on a weekly basis. Every week, they are tracking the progress or non-progress of the runner. Why? Because the coaches want their athletes to meet their goals when it comes time to compete. It makes no sense to have great ideas and no tracking.

When you ship a package, you track those boxes that have valuable items in them to make sure that they arrive at their destination on time. The same is true in life. If you want to get somewhere by the time you turn a certain age, then you've got to track your progress. Track your growth. Track your success. Track your weaknesses. Track your strength.

Life's blessings don't come to us in a box called "potential." The great things in life come with work, a plan, and good tracking. No matter what your goals are, take the time to write them down. If you are trying to lose weight or gain muscle mass, write down your goal weight. Work hard everyday to make it happen. And then reward yourself when you've reached your goal. Indeed, all things are possible...but how hard are you willing to work for them?

Every day you should water the garden of your goals. Until you focus on your future, your future will not focus on you. ■

CHALLENGE

Name your short-term and long-term goals. Start with the end in mind and celebrate when you reach certain milestones. The only way to change your tomorrow is to work hard today.

EXERCISE

I set goals every school year. ☐ Yes ☐ No

I achieve most goals that I set. ☐ Yes ☐ No

_____stops me from setting or achieving my goals.

" Mentors guide us and protect

us from becoming repeat offenders.

Experience only teaches you how

to protect yourself later. "

34

MENTORSHIP VS. EXPERIENCE
DON'T BE AFRAID TO ASK FOR HELP

We learn about life in two ways—either from mentors or by experience. Mentors care enough to help you. Experience will take you to the bottom in order to get you to the top. Mentors understand the end goal and try to help you to avoid pain. Experience takes pain and turns it into purpose. Which do you run to when you want to learn? Do you have a mentor or do you only learn by experience?

Experience is the hardest way to "get it," but so many of us love to climb up the rough side of the mountain. Especially when we are young, we feel that nobody knows what we are going through, so we learn the hard way. Many young men aren't comfortable or are too proud to learn from someone who has experienced the journey.

I believe that we as men can have too much pride feeling like we have to do things on our own. Personally, I was always a little pridoful and independent as a child. I didn't really think others could mentor me. In fact, I didn't think I needed to be mentored. But when I finally found my mentor, I realized that just listening to him could save me a lot of heartache and pain.

You know what I mean. It's like setting up a DVD player or putting together a piece of furniture. Most men do not like to pick up the manual because we assume that we have it under control. So it takes us five hours to put together something that would've only taken 15 minutes.

We tend to be stubborn. It starts when we're children. We want to color the book ourselves. We want to figure it out on our own. And when we are left by ourselves, we rarely ask for help.

The mentor in your life is like the manual to the furniture. His purpose is to instruct you so that you don't waste time trying to do something that won't work in the end. Mentors guide us and protect us from becoming repeat offenders. Experience only teaches you how to protect yourself later. Experience, if it is not combined with mentorship, can cause frustration, aggravation, and delay. ▪

CHALLENGE

We all have the ability to learn from someone else. We ask our basketball coach to teach us techniques to become better ball players. We ask a librarian to help us find a book instead of spending all day looking on our own.

EXERCISE

Is having a mentor beneficial in my life? ☐ Yes ☐ No

I would be willing to open myself up for coaching from a mentor. ☐ Yes ☐ No

" What if you lived everyday

like your dreams could really come

true? The greatest gift we have as

humans is our ability to imagine.

If you can think it,

you can become it. "

35

DWELL IN POSSIBILITY
ANYTHING IS POSSIBLE IF YOU CAN IMAGINE IT

All things are possible. Every idea is attainable. In fact, you can become anything that you set your mind to become, but do you really believe that? Are you living every day full of possibility, or are you living every day full of pessimism?

What if you lived everyday like your dreams could really come true? What if you really could earn that degree? What if the NBA did sign you in the next three years? The greatest gift we have as humans is our ability to imagine. If you can think it, you can become it.

I encourage you to begin each day with a new "what if." What if you could become a banker or a lawyer? What if the characters you read about or watch in a film are actually showing you who you can become? What if you really could buy your mother a new house someday? What if? The more you dwell in possibility, the greater your imagination becomes.

I would watch *The Cosby Show* and think, What if I could become a great father like Dr. Huxtable? What if I made enough money to provide for my family? Remember, I didn't have many models in my life, so the only way I could dream out loud was to see it on the television. But I also decided to make it happen in my life. Now that I'm older, I can thankfully say that I have become the father I could only see in my imagination. I have become the provider that I once saw on television.

What's my point? All things are possible. If we can dream it, we can become it.

What if you dwelled, for a day, in possibility? What if you dreamt about the impossible and then worked to make it happen? Walt Disney, Steve Jobs, Bill Gates, and Barack Obama surely had dreams to become great people. I'm sure they had hurdles and moments of discouragement. But one day, they built their imaginations up enough to believe that it could happen. ▪

CHALLENGE

Before you can believe in anyone else's dreams, believe in your own. Dare to dream, and work as if you know it's going to work.

EXERCISE

What dreams do you hold onto?

_____

_____

_____

What is stopping you from fulfilling those dreams?

_____

_____

_____

I choose to dwell in this possibility: _____

_____

_____

"Whether we realize it or not,

life is about seasons: learn, grow,

love, and laugh."

36

THE FOUR SEASONS
LEARN, GROW, LOVE, LAUGH

When I was a kid, I loved to watch the seasons change. Winter. Spring. Summer. Fall. As a child, I loved them all! After the leaves fell, I remember going out to rake the yard. The best memory was not raking them, but jumping in the pile at the end of the day. That was a fun time! The seasons were changing, and that's exactly what happened in my life.

Whether we realize it or not, life is about seasons. Instead of using spring, summer, fall, and winter, I want to talk about the four seasons of life that relate to all of us: learn, grow, love, and laugh.

Learn: The learning season is where we start, but it is also a never-ending opportunity in life. Learning helps you to build confidence. It makes you more disciplined. It expands and broadens your horizons. For most of us, learning helps us to get our jobs! So learning is important. But even after high school and college, you will come back around to seasons of learning. Remember: the seasons always change from year to year.

Grow: The growth season is about stretching. We can't wear the clothes we used to wear as infants because our bodies outgrew them. If we never outgrew anything in life, then we'd be stuck in those baby clothes forever. In all things we must grow: mentally, spiritually, physically, intellectually, etc. Of course, stretching can hurt. And the more we stretch, the more it can hurt. But don't resist the pain. In order to grow, we've got to endure this season of stretching. Otherwise, we're going to look awfully foolish in those baby clothes!

Love: All of us need love, both with that special someone and in our family life. One day, you may be a father. One day, you may be a grandfather. So this season will constantly repeat itself. But here's the thing about love that we must understand. Love is not about fluttering feelings and butterflies in your stomach. Sure, those things do happen at first, but true love is a commitment. True love will survive those moments when you are not as excited today as you were yesterday. In every relationship, there will be highs and lows. But your job is to focus on finding a balance in your love season. Don't leave the love when and if the excitement goes away. Instead, find new ways to show your love. Find new places to go to give new life to your love. If your love means the world to you, then be willing to work through this season—no matter how tough love gets.

Laugh: Laughter is medicine for the soul. When we don't laugh, our bodies don't get the medicine they need to heal. Laughing will help your spirit. It will boost your morale. It will help you not to take life too seriously. If you can laugh your way through it, you can make it through anything. ■

CHALLENGE

Don't be afraid to laugh, love, learn, and grow.

EXERCISE

Which season are you in right now?

_____

_____

_____

Which season do you need to work on?

_____

_____

_____

Why does that season need more work?

_____

_____

_____

Once you answer these questions, make it a daily practice to focus on certain seasons in your life.

_____

_____

_____

66 Learn to transform

your fear into fearlessness.

The true winners in life

are those who

meet every opportunity

with determination. 99

37

AFRAID TO LOSE, DETERMINED TO WIN

WE HAVE THE CHOICE TO DECIDE

Michael Jordan is one of the best basketball players who ever lived. I remember watching Jordan as a kid and wishing I could play like him. But I also remember the 1991 Pistons vs. Bulls game. That year, Chicago won their first of six championships, and as a Pistons fan, for me it was the end of a great era in Motown basketball.

As I watched the game, I remember thinking, Who will take the last shot? Are the Pistons even trying? And then the commentator said something like, "They aren't playing to win; they are playing not to lose."

You know, a lot of us live our lives this way. We play it safe. We assume the worst. We don't enter the ring to become champions; we are just excited to be in the ring. But do you really think that's the best way to look at life? My belief is simple. If you are going to play, you might as well be determined to win. If you are afraid of anything, you should be afraid of what would happen if you didn't step out and do it.

It makes no sense to prepare for a championship

and coast along. Why would you go all the way to the Olympics to play it safe? If you are going to become a New York Times Bestseller, you've got to take each sentence seriously. If you want to be the greatest dad, you've got to be determined to win your child's love. Learn to transform your fear into fearlessness. The true winners in life are those who meet every opportunity with determination.

Focus on these words: I am determined not to give up. I am determined to succeed. I may not win every game, but I intend to win the tournament. I am determined to graduate. I am determined to live a positive life of integrity. I am determined to provide for my family.

This determination will bring you greater results. Determination changes your mentality. It helps you to look at every shot like Michael Jordan did: life or death. It didn't matter that Jordan scored the most points or that the Bulls had a two-point lead or a 30-point lead. When you are determined, you stick your chest out and fight hard until the end.

If you want to succeed in life, you've got to be determined to win. You have to see yourself winning before you step out on the court of life. Don't become one of the guys who doubts himself out of the race. In their minds, it was easier to do nothing than to try and fail. In my mind, you've already failed if you haven't tried. ▪

CHALLENGE

Are you afraid to lose or determined to win? If you are determined to win, what things need to change in your life? What will help you to become a more determined man?

EXERCISE

_____is an

example of living a life afraid to lose.

_____is an

example of living a life determined to win.

" Nobody knows it all.

We give and we take.

We live and we learn. And the more

we live, the more we grow. "

38

LEARNING IS A STEP-BY-STEP PROCESS
THE THING THAT LEADS TO THE THING

My daughter used to carry her "Connect the Dots" book around everywhere. The goal was easy—figure out the big picture after the dots were connected. What began as a simple goal became increasingly difficult on each page. My daughter, however, is a persistent young lady! She would sit in the back seat and draw, draw, draw until she got it! She didn't get flustered or frustrated. She set her eye on the prize, and she enjoyed the challenge.

Watching her enjoy the game, I learned that life is not a straight line. Life is all about connecting the dots...dot by dot and line by line. Every experience is a dot. Every decision is a line. Good or bad, our experiences offer us lessons about life.

I've learned to enjoy the connect-the-dots process of life. One dot will lead you to another dot. I've learned not to be in such a rush that I don't take the time to really "get it" before I move from one dot to the next. The choice to attend the best school could lead you to meet your best friend, who will then introduce you to the best boss you've ever had. Another relationship could lead you down a dark path. But what if, at the end of it, there is a ray of sunshine? What if certain events or experiences that seem random are actually the dots that connect us to our true purpose?

I've interviewed a lot of people during my years with a major corporation. During those interviews, I hear interviewees ask, "Why can't I get the job? Why can't I get the promotion?" They are upset because they want an immediate promotion, but they haven't earned their first paycheck! Patience, my brother! Patience. All things worth having are worth waiting for. Enjoy the journey and don't rush through life.

Every job I had in the beginning of my journey had nothing to do with the job I have now. I worked at a bakery, a car wash, a tailor shop, a fast food joint—I did it all. And while I thought they had nothing to do with each other, I realize now that each job taught me different skills that I now use for the job I currently hold. It was all a process.

You can't go from A to Z without connecting all those dots in between. Don't underestimate the position you hold today. Maybe you're picking up valuable lessons along the way that will help you to connect the dots in life. When we understand the process, we free ourselves from the pressure to know it all. Nobody knows it all. We give and we take. We live and we learn. And the more we live, the more we grow. ■

CHALLENGE

Think about every job you've ever had. Place them under a microscope. How did they improve you? What skills did you learn? Are you better for them? If so, then be thankful for the process!

EXERCISE

List three instances when you learned something and were able to apply it to another time in your life.

1.

_____

_____

_____

2.

_____

_____

_____

3.

_____

_____

_____

"As young men, we have to identify

a cluster of people who we care about.

...Wherever that community is,

we have to cherish it. Honor it.

Be grateful for it."

39

FRIENDS
DON'T TAKE THEM FOR GRANTED

Who are your friends? How do you know? Are you the kind of person who befriends everyone? Or are you the kind who lives in isolation? No matter where you are on the spectrum, realize that we all need close friends.

Most of the people we meet in life are just associates. We know them temporarily, but they aren't friends. Friends are people we can trust. Friends are people we can call at any time of the day and we know they will reach back out to us. True friends last a lifetime. Friends will be there with you through the thick and the thin. Real friends are treasures—so don't live your life without being open to friendship.

In the Fall of 2012, I lost one of my best friends. He was only in his forties, but he passed away suddenly. It devastated me. He was there when my child was born. He was with me during difficult relationships. He stuck with me even after I advanced in my career. He was my ride-or-die friend. He taught me more than any professor did. Our bond to one another transcended time and space. If he needed me, I was there. If I needed him, he was there.

Friends are our greatest teachers, and many of us don't realize how important friendship is. As the generations change, we tend to value people less and less. We use the computer for everything. Technology has tainted us. We text. We rarely ever call. Writing letters has become a lost art. Going out to eat and just having a conversation is old news. Our ability to connect has suffered. Why? Because we have lost value in friendship.

As young men, we have to identify a cluster of people who we care about. Maybe that happens in a fraternity, in a church, or in our families—but wherever that community is, we have to cherish it. Honor it. Be grateful for it. Take time this week to thank each of your friends for being in your life. Never underestimate the people who are with you. You just may look up one day and discover they aren't there any more. ▪

CHALLENGE

If you want to have a friend, be a friend. Many times we look for people to be for us what we aren't for others. Identify your weaknesses. Improve your friendliness. The harder you work on yourself, the more likely someone will be willing to work with you.

EXERCISE

Who is your best friend?

_____

_____

What do you admire about him or her?

_____

_____

Do you have any friends who are no longer here with you?

_____

_____

If so, what do you miss about them?

_____

_____

What do you wish you had said to them or done for them while they were still around?

_____

_____

" When it's your turn to get in

the game, will you blame it on

your environment or will you

choose to break the cycle and chart

your own path? "

40

YOU GOT NEXT
BREAKING THE CYCLE

Milton Brooks, my grandfather. He was known for hard work, street savvy, and excessive women. Stories from my family speak of his stellar work ethic, amazing sense of humor, and love for the streets. Although he passed away a few years ago, he is somewhat of a legend to those who had the pleasure of knowing him. My memories of my grandfather aren't filled with baseball games or a game of checkers in the park. The memories are filled with him dropping me and my cousins off with one of his many girlfriends while he and his buddies hung out.

Reginald Bean, my father. A hard working, 30-year veteran of the automobile industry. My father was known for his intellect, business acumen, and love for a constant rotation of women. As a kid, memories of my father are not filled with playful days in the park or a consistent presence at my school for parent teacher conferences. Instead my only memories are those from the parties he would host or learning how to drive at the age of thirteen because he would drink so excessively that he would pass out in the driver's seat for hours.

Now it's my turn: I'm up next. It's my shot at manhood, fatherhood, and to lead a family. Now keep in mind that most of the men who I saw as a young person were similar in behavior to my father and grandfather. When it was my turn to step into the role of "man" and lead a family, I emulated what I saw growing up and failed miserably. I married at the age of 23 and divorced ten years later because I allowed what I was taught as a child to continue living. In other words, I allowed the cycle of dysfunction and false information to exist in my life.

We all are products of our environments, we emulate both positive and negative behavior. But it's up to us to recognize the patterns and decide the paths and patterns that we will continue or the cycles we will break in our lives. When it's your turn to get in the game, will you blame it on your environment or will you choose to break the cycle and chart your own path?

The choice is yours. This life is yours. Make the most of it! ▪

CHALLENGE

Eventually, you will be next. You will have the opportunity to lead. How will you lead? Will you keep the tradition going or will you step up and break the cycle?

EXERCISE

My family has a negative cycle of _____
_____ that I would like to break.

My family has a positive cycle of _____
_____ that I would like to continue.

When it's my turn, I will create _____
_____
new cycle for my kids, grandkids, and community.

REGINALD BEAN
DIRECTOR-MULTICULTURAL MARKETING
COCA-COLA BOTTLING CO CONSOLIDATED

Reginald Bean is the Director of Multicultural Marketing with Coca-Cola bottling. In his role, Reginald is responsible for the development and implementation of marketing programs that promote and sustain cultural awareness, inclusion, equity, and respect within the African American, Hispanic/Latino, and Asian American cultures.

Reginald began his career with Coca-Cola Consolidated in 1999, when he joined the company in territory sales. He held several positions within Coca Cola including Strategic Planning Analyst, Director of Finance-Operations, and Director of Sales Analytics. Prior to joining Coca-Cola Consolidated, Reginald served his country in the US Army for seven years where he participated in several international desert and urban training missions.

Reginald holds a Bachelor in Operations Management from DeVry University. Reginald enthusiastically serves on the board of directors for The Urban League of Central Carolinas, The Police Activities League, and the National Academy of Finance. Reginald shares lives journey with a wonderful wife, Shavonda, and daughter Arden. He enjoys numerous physical activities including working out and golf. Lastly, Reginald's hobbies include reading, cooking, and performing as a garage DJ. ■

REGINALD BEAN'S INVIGORATING SPEECHES MOTIVATE YOUNG MINDS

Reginald Bean founded Ideas In Motion in 2012 with the purpose of using his journey, passion and speaking ability to motivate young minds. When you book Reginald to speak for your organization, you will begin a partnership that will motivate your students, athletes and staff to push toward optimal production. Reginald is available to speak on topics including but not limited to:

- Purpose
- From Hobby to Passion
- Goal Setting
- Self Development
- Thriving through Transition
  (middle school to high school, high school
  to college, college to work life, incarceration to freedom
- Career Development

BOOK REGINALD TODAY!

877-318-8638
Reginaldbean@gmail.com
Twitter: @reginaldbean
Facebook: facebook.com/Reginald.Bean

To order additional copies or learn more,
please visit: www.40-Lessons.com

Made in the USA
Charleston, SC
07 January 2014